Love food

lose weight

igloobooks

igloobooks

Published in 2015
by Igloo Books Ltd
Cottage Farm
Sywell
NN6 0BJ
www.igloobooks.com

Food photography and recipe development: © Stockfood, The Food Media Agency
Front cover images: © Stockfood, The Food Media Agency (top left and top right); iStock (main image and top middle)
Back inside flap: iStock

Designed by Stephen Jorgensen
Edited by Natalie Baker

LEO002 1015
2 4 6 8 10 9 7 5 3 1
ISBN 978-1-78557-014-8

Printed and manufactured in China

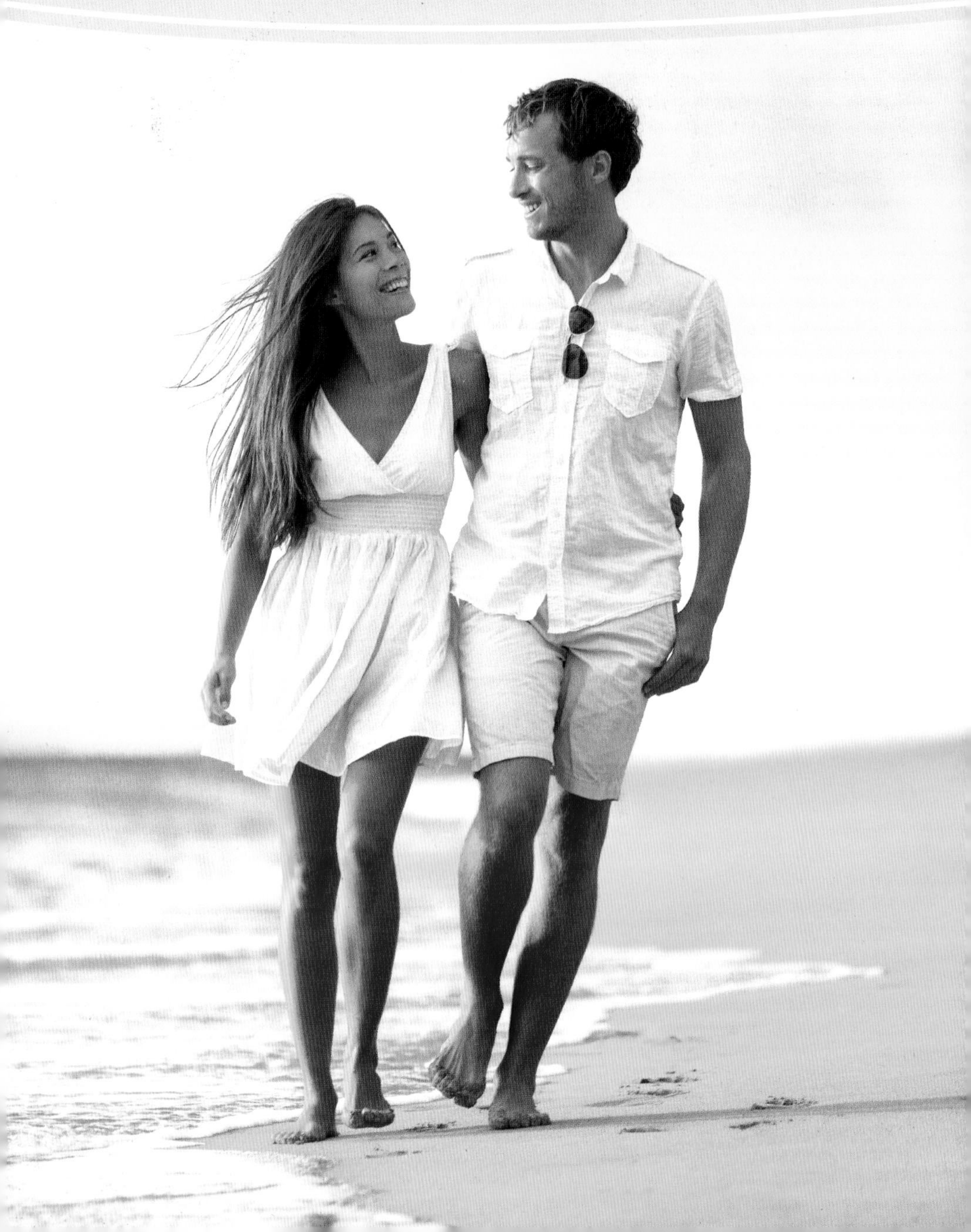

Contents

The spice of life

Some fad diets limit you to just a small range of foods, which can quickly become boring. A good diet is one that allows you to try a wide range of different foods. This book shows you how to take some basic healthy ingredients, such as wholegrains and vegetables, and turn them into a huge variety of mouth-watering dishes. Losing weight has never been so delicious!

Introduction

Nearly all of us have decided to lose weight at one point or another. For most people, that means trying a diet and there are plenty to choose from: vegan, Paleolithic, macrobiotic, juice-based, sugar-free, gluten-free – the list is endless! Even though some people find success with these diets, they can seem like hard work and not much fun. After all, who wants to live on carrot sticks and brown rice every day?

Recipe for success

Study after study has shown that the majority of people who lose weight on a diet will put it back on within a few years, if not sooner. Some crash diets offer a quick way to lose weight, but when the diet is finished, the pounds pile back on. If you want to keep weight off, you'll need to change your lifestyle in a way that you can keep up for the long term.

Out with the bad, in with the good

You'll have the best chance of sticking to a diet if it focuses on foods that you actually like! Structure your everyday diet around delicious, healthy foods and gradually eliminate the unhealthy parts of your diet, such as simple carbs, fatty meats, refined sugars and processed foods.

Eat Well, Live Long

Eating well isn't just about staying slim or looking good. Your daily diet affects your overall health in ways that you may not even have realised. There's a lot of truth to the expression, 'you are what you eat'! A healthy diet based around fresh, unprocessed, nutritious foods can lower your risk for conditions such as obesity, high blood pressure, heart attack, diabetes, stroke and even some types of cancer.

Flashback

Until the last century or so, most people ate fairly healthily. Meat was expensive, so for all but the richest people, vegetables and grains made up the bulk of their diet. The closest thing to a processed food would have been the bread that you made yourself from flour, yeast, water and salt.

Of course, these diets still had their downsides. Before the days of air freight, refrigeration and chemical preservatives, people were limited to what was local and in season, so there was less variety. Cooking also took up more of people's time than it does now. These days, our supermarket shelves are filled with appealing, easy-to-prepare food from around the world, 365 days a year. But all this convenience and variety can sometimes come at a price.

Healthy societies

Some regions have long put healthy eating at the core of their cultural identity. For example, the traditional diet of countries bordering the Mediterranean Sea, such as Italy, Greece and Spain, is largely based on vegetables, fruits, nuts, beans, wholegrains, olive oil and fish. One study showed that this diet gave people a 30 per cent lower risk of heart disease and stroke.

The Good, the Bad and the Ugly

The last 50 years or so have seen a revolution in the way we eat. Many families no longer have a wife or mother who stays at home to cook and clean. Our busy lives mean that meals often have to be prepared in a hurry, or eaten on the go. Processed foods such as ready meals and fast food have made our lives much more convenient, but they are rarely as nutritious as a home-made meal cooked from fresh ingredients.

Walk through the aisles of any supermarket and you'll see a vast array of cakes, cereals, sauces, soups, prepared meals and snacks. These foods are often cheaper than fresh fruit and vegetables and they need little or no preparation. However, they are often high in calories, as well as refined sugar, salt or fat.

Getting it right

A healthy diet is one that reduces the intake of refined sugars, simple carbs, fatty meats and alcohol. Eating too much of these foods can cause obesity, which can lead to other conditions, such as diabetes. Many scientists believe that diets high in simple carbs, such as those found in fruit or white bread, can lead to an increased risk of diabetes. Studies have shown that eating too much refined sugar can increase the risk of heart disease.

Hitting the sweet spot

Food manufacturers want us to buy their products, so they try to find just the right formula that will keep us coming back for more. Unfortunately, this can mean replacing natural ingredients with synthetic additives that mimic the sweet, salty or fatty tastes we love. Many processed foods are full of synthetic ingredients such as aspartame and high fructose corn syrup. Others use genetically modified foods.

Reading Food Labels

There's one good thing about processed foods: by law, they have to be clearly labelled, so you know exactly what's in them. However, there are so many different types of labels that you need to be savvy to make sure you're getting the healthiest food possible.
Here are a few tips:

- The 'suggested serving size' is often smaller than the servings you're used to. When you get home, weigh it out to see what it looks like.

- Nutrition information is also calculated per 100 grams. You may not plan to eat exactly 100 grams of whatever it is, but it is a useful way to compare nutrition information for two different products.

- Some foods have 'traffic light' labels on the front that show you at a glance whether they are high in sugar, fat, salt, carbs and energy: red for high, amber for medium and green for low.

- The healthiest foods often contain the fewest ingredients. If the ingredients list is made up of dozens of names you don't even recognise, avoid it.

- Drinks often contain a lot of sugar, so read labels carefully.

- Don't be fooled by packaging that says 'low fat' or 'low carb'. Some of these foods have other ingredients added to make up for what's missing. For example, some foods labelled 'low fat' have a lot of added sugar.

Hidden sugar

Processed foods often contain a lot of added sugar, but you'll need to use your detective skills to find it. Added sugar can go by many names, including high fructose corn syrup, malt syrup, inverted sugar, honey, agave and molasses. Also watch out for glucose, dextrose and pretty much everything ending in '-ose'. Because ingredients are listed in order of weight, splitting the added sugar into half a dozen different ingredients pushes them lower down the list, making the product look healthier than it really is.

How Your Body Works

Your body is an amazing machine. It takes in whatever you feed it, extracts the useful nutrients, converts calories into energy and gets rid of whatever you don't need. It can cope with a lot, but it's not indestructible. Overloading your body with the wrong types of food can lead to serious health problems.

Digesting your food

When you eat, the food moves through your digestive system, where strong acids and muscle contractions break it down into a mush. Nutrients and water in the food are absorbed into the bloodstream.

Your body has many ways of getting rid of waste products. The kidneys filter out toxins from the blood and turn them into urine, which you then pass out of your body. Your skin gets rid of salts and sugars when you sweat. The large intestine turns food waste and old body cells into faeces.

Look after your liver

Your liver filters out toxins from the blood. It is very resilient, but every time it filters alcohol, some of its cells die. If you drink too much alcohol over a long period of time, your liver can become permanently damaged. Another serious condition, called fatty liver disease, is caused by a build-up of fatty cells in the liver, which is more common in people who are overweight or obese.

Overload!

Some foods can overload the body's natural waste management systems. For example, salt is often found in large quantities in processed foods. Eating too much salt makes it harder for your kidneys to remove water from the blood, causing high blood pressure.

Losing the Pounds

If you want to lose weight, you need to eat less and exercise more. Sounds simple, right? The tricky part is discovering how many calories you normally burn and working out a diet that puts your intake below that. The NHS recommends a daily intake of 2,000 calories for women and 2,500 calories for men. However, this can vary a lot, depending on your age, size, genes, level of physical activity and many other factors.

It takes time

For most people, improving their diet and losing weight is a long-term goal rather than a quick fix. Many doctors recommend a target loss of between one and two pounds a week. To do this you'll need to consume no more than 1,400 calories per day for women and 1,900 for men. This doesn't necessarily mean eating less, just eating healthier. For example, the average packet of crisps weighs 35 grams and contains about 180 calories. The same amount of steamed broccoli has only 60 calories or so and it is packed with nutrients.

Doing it safely

Losing weight is just like any other major lifestyle change – you need to be ready for it. Even if you're in good health, you should still talk to your GP before you start. He or she can make sure your body can cope with a change in diet and maybe even provide some useful tips.

How weight loss works

When you eat more calories than your body uses up, you will gain weight. The body stores extra calories as fat cells, in case their energy is needed later. Over time, these extra fat cells build up and make you fat. If you eat fewer calories than your body uses, it will burn those fat cells to get the energy you need, causing you to lose weight.

Exercise and Stress Management

Exercise is an important part of any weight-loss plan. You can change your diet to reduce your calorie intake, but exercise will help you burn off more of what you eat. In addition, regular exercise has other health benefits. It can help keep your heart and lungs healthy, as well as releasing hormones that make you feel happier.

High-impact, low-impact

You'll get the most benefit out of exercise that gets your blood pumping. Running, cycling, spinning and kick-boxing are great ways to burn calories and, as they get you breathing hard, they'll improve your overall cardiovascular health.

You may not want to do vigorous exercise every day, so try to mix it up: a low-impact activity such as swimming can give your knees a bit of a rest. Yoga and pilates are a great way to keep your body strong and flexible.

Keep moving

Even if you're not hitting the treadmill, it's still important to keep moving. Take the stairs whenever you can, park further away than you're used to, walk rather than drive for short journeys and don't be afraid to dance around the room if the mood takes you. These little bits of activity really add up – even an hour of hoovering burns around 200 calories!

Think yourself thin

Many people today are turning to meditation and mindfulness to help them lose weight. These practices focus your attention in order to find calm and clarity. Meditating won't burn calories, but it can lower high blood pressure and manage stress (which is a reason some people overeat). Some studies have shown that practising mindful eating can help to control cravings and comfort eating.

Healthy Food Swaps

Changing your diet to be healthier may seem like a big challenge, but it's less daunting if you take it one step at a time. Keep a food diary and make a list of any foods you eat that are high in calories, fat, salt or sugars. Then, gradually replace these foods with similar options that pack more of a nutritional punch.

Artificial sweeteners

Eating too much refined sugar can cause health problems, but what's the best replacement? There are many different natural sweeteners on the market. Some of them, like coconut sugar and agave nectar, are more natural than refined sugar and have some nutrients. But they are still full of sugar, so you should use them only sparingly. Maple syrup has useful minerals and less sucrose per gram than refined sugar. A better option is stevia, a natural plant-based sweetener that has zero calories and can reduce blood pressure.

Get rid of...	...and replace it with:
beef mince	turkey mince
biscuits	oatcakes and rice cakes
Cheddar cheese	reduced-fat cheese or naturally low-fat cheeses such as cottage cheese
creamy or cheesy sauces	tomato or vegetable-based sauces
crisps	nuts or dried fruit (look for unsalted varieties with no added sugar and sulphur dioxide)
fatty cuts of meat	tofu or lean meats such as fish or skinless chicken breast
mayonnaise	mashed avocado
milk chocolate	dark chocolate (with a high cocoa content)
semi-skimmed or whole milk	skimmed milk, almond milk, rice milk, oat milk or soya milk
sugary breakfast cereal	wholegrain cereal or home-made porridge and granola (sprinkle with berries or dried fruit instead of sugar)
sugary fizzy drinks	water, or a small amount of fruit juice mixed with sparkling water
table salt	small amounts of sea salt and fresh herbs and spices
white bread	wholegrain bread (including gluten-free bread)
white rice (basmati, long grain, etc)	brown rice and wild rice

Portion Control

Don't get discouraged if some of your much-loved foods appeared on the list of 'get rid of' items. You don't have to cut out all of these foods to lose weight, as long as you eat them in moderation. This may mean saving them for occasional treats or rewards. But even if you already have a diet that's full of the healthier options, you'll have to eat less of them if you want to lose weight. If you're aiming for that 1,400-calorie daily limit, you'll probably have to reduce portion sizes.

Here are some tips for keeping portions under control:

- To find out how big a portion should be, download a chart giving easy examples for familiar foods. For example, a serving of chicken should be about the size of a deck of cards.

- Use a smaller plate. It sounds crazy, but scientific studies have shown that we are more likely to serve and eat bigger portions if we use bigger dishes.

- Drink a glass of water before every meal. It will make you feel full more quickly, so you'll eat less.

- Instead of bringing the serving dish to the table, dish out a moderate portion in the kitchen. You'll be less likely to go back for seconds.

- Eat slowly. Chewing your food properly is great for digestion.

Home-made ready meals

At the weekend, why not make a big batch of soup, veggie chilli, turkey bolognese sauce or healthy curry? All of these dishes freeze well, so weigh out individual portions and freeze them. Then, if you have a day where you're too tired or don't have time to cook, you'll have a healthy, portion-controlled ready meal in your freezer. Steam some veggies and cook some brown rice or wholegrain pasta to serve alongside. Easy-peasy!

Eating Out

Sharing a meal with friends is always fun and it's even better when you don't have to cook! But sticking to a healthy diet while eating out can be tricky. Food at restaurants is often high in fat and calories, and when you're having a good time it's easy to overindulge. Try to make takeaways or meals out a rare treat rather than a weekly ritual.

Here are some tips for staying healthy when you eat out:

- Choose a restaurant or cafe with a reputation for healthy food. Some modern chains are becoming known for their fresh ingredients and healthy options.

- Say 'no thanks' to the basket of bread on the table. Having a small, healthy snack before you go out may make it easier to avoid filling up on bread or dips.

- Don't be embarrassed to ask questions about the menu, or to request small changes, such as steamed vegetables instead of sautéed.

- Watch out for sauces and salad dressings; they are often high in calories. Ask to have them served on the side, and use sparingly.

- Why not order a salad or a starter as your main meal? You can ask for it to be brought out with the main courses. Many restaurants offer smaller portions of their main meals as a starter. Choose one of these and get a side of steamed vegetables to complete the meal.

- It's not just the ingredients that matter. Look for dishes that are cooked in a healthy way, such as fish that is baked rather than fried.

Two in one

When eating out, stick to your portion control. Some restaurant meals are big enough for two! Eat only as much as you'd eat at home, and don't feel bad if you don't clear your plate. Ask to have the leftovers wrapped up. That's your packed lunch for the next day sorted!

Breakfasts and Brunches

When you're trying to lose weight, it can be tempting to skip breakfast. But this can leave you hungry and tired by mid-morning, making you more likely to snack. It's much better to start the day right, with a healthy, nutritious breakfast that will keep you going all the way until lunch.

Many of us eat packaged cereals, or toast with butter and jam – both of which can be high in sugar and sometimes fat, too. These breakfasts are quick and easy, making them tempting when we're in a rush. But there are much better alternatives that are also quick to prepare.

Eggs have had bad press in the past, but they're rich in protein and are a great way to start the day. It takes hardly any time to make an omelette in the morning. To make it healthier, ditch one of the egg yolks and replace ham and Cheddar with spinach and goats' cheese.

Bircher Muesli

Serves: 4 / Preparation time: 10 minutes + overnight
Calories per portion: 366

Ingredients

100 g / 3 ½ oz / 2 ½ cups rolled oats

100 g / 3 ½ oz / ⅔ cup raisins

2 tbsp flaked (slivered) almonds

2 tbsp golden flaxseeds

500 ml / 18 fl. oz / 2 cups unsweetened
almond milk

250 ml / 9 fl. oz / 1 cup light coconut milk

2 Gala apples, cored and sliced

Method

1. Combine the oats, raisins, almonds,
   flaxseeds and both milks in a large
   mixing bowl.

2. Stir well, cover loosely and chill overnight.

3. Divide the muesli between bowls and stir in
   the apple before serving.

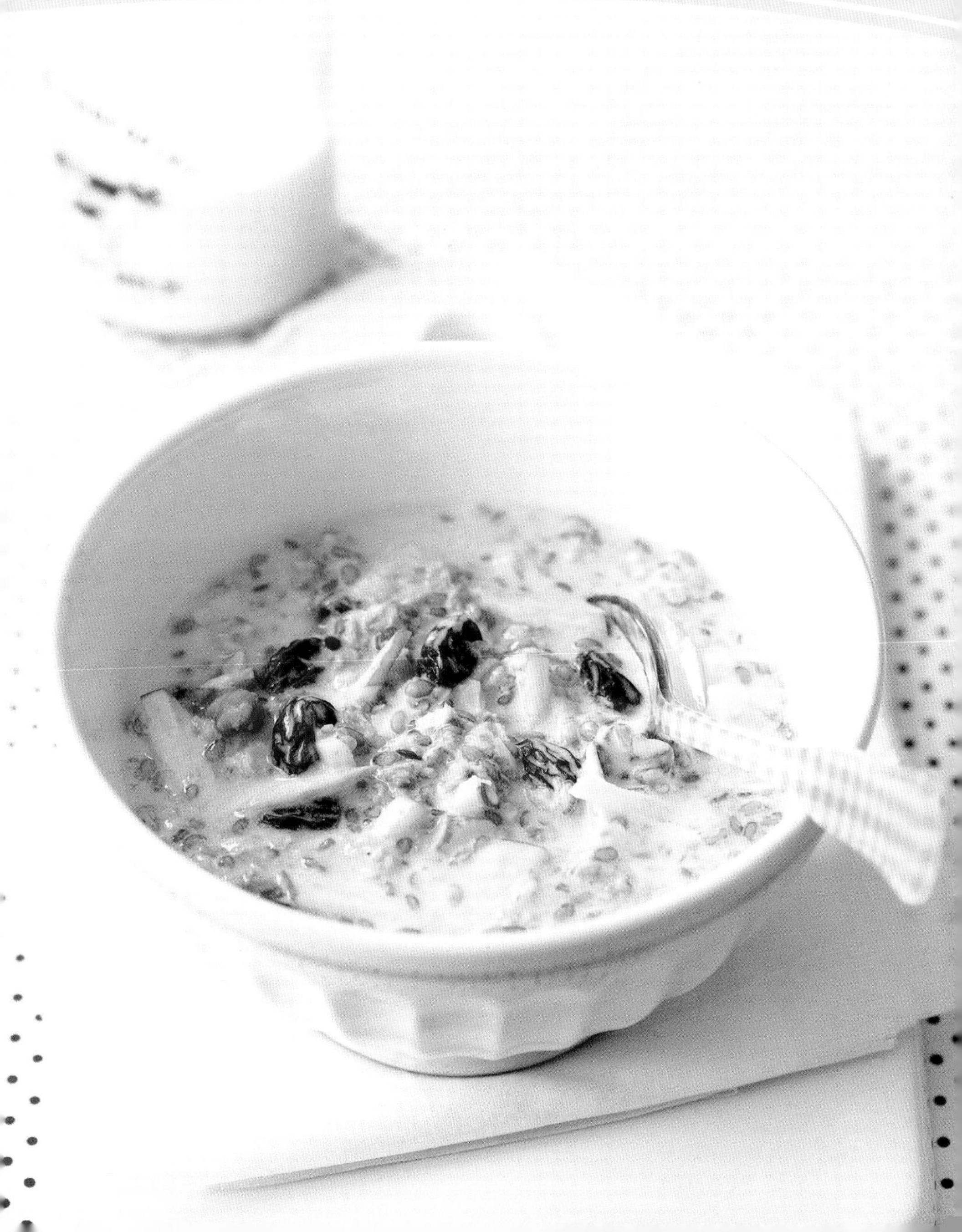

Poached Eggs on Potato Cakes

Serves: 4 / Preparation time: 15 minutes

Cooking time: 30 minutes / Calories per portion: 353

Ingredients

750 g / 1 lb 10 oz / 5 cups Maris Piper potatoes, peeled and diced

140 g / 5 oz / 2 cups Savoy cabbage, shredded

2 tbsp coconut oil

1 tbsp cornflour (cornstarch), plus extra for dusting

3 tbsp avocado oil

2 tbsp white wine vinegar

4 medium eggs

55 g / 2 oz / 1 cup mixed leaf salad, to serve

a large handful of cress, to serve

salt and freshly ground black pepper

Method

1. Cook the potatoes in a large saucepan of salted, boiling water for 15 minutes until almost tender to the point of a knife. Just before draining, add the cabbage and cook for a further 2 minutes until softened.

2. Drain well and leave to steam dry for a few minutes. Add the coconut oil and cornflour, mashing well until smooth. Season generously with salt and pepper.

3. Heat the avocado oil in a large sauté pan set over a medium heat until hot. Shape the potato mixture into cakes and dust both sides with cornflour, shaking off the excess.

4. Sauté the potato cakes for 3–4 minutes, until golden underneath. Flip and cook for a further 2–3 minutes until golden.

5. Meanwhile, stir the white wine vinegar into a large saucepan of simmering water. Poach the eggs for 3 minutes. Remove with a slotted spoon and drain on kitchen paper.

6. Serve the eggs on top of the cakes, garnished with salad and cress on the side.

Pear and Pancetta Muffins

Makes: 12 / Preparation time: 10 minutes

Cooking time: 30 minutes / Calories per portion: 229

Ingredients

2 tbsp potato flour

½ tsp gluten-free baking powder

300 g / 11 oz / 2 cups gluten-free plain
(all-purpose) flour, sifted

½ tsp bicarbonate of (baking) soda

150 ml / 5 fl. oz / ⅔ cup avocado oil

150 ml / 5 fl. oz / ⅔ cup unsweetened
almond milk

2 small Rocha pears, cored and diced

100 g / 3 ½ oz / ⅔ cup pancetta, diced

a small handful of pea shoots, to garnish

225 g / 8 oz / 1 cup coconut milk yoghurt

salt

Method

1. Preheat the oven to 180°C (160°C fan) /
   350F / gas 4. Line a 12-hole muffin tray
   with paper cases.

2. Whisk together the potato flour, baking
   powder and 55 ml / 2 fl. oz / ¼ cup of tepid
   water in a small bowl.

3. Combine the plain flour, bicarbonate of
   soda and a pinch of salt in a large mixing
   bowl, stirring well.

4. Whisk together the avocado oil and almond
   milk in a mixing jug. Pour into the dry
   ingredients along with the prepared potato
   flour mixture and combine with a spatula,
   taking care not to over-mix.

5. Add the pear and pancetta and mix again
   briefly. Divide the batter between the cases
   and bake for 20–25 minutes until golden
   and risen on top.

6. Remove to a wire rack to cool. Top with
   coconut milk yoghurt and pea shoots
   when serving.

Home-made Granola

Serves: 4 / Preparation time: 5 minutes
Cooking time: 30 minutes / Calories per portion: 493

Ingredients

non-fat cooking spray
125 g / 4 ½ oz / 3 cups rolled oats
1 tsp ground cinnamon
¼ tsp salt
1 tbsp ground flaxseed
75 g / 3 oz / ¾ cup whole almonds
100 g / 3 ½ oz / ⅔ cup raisins
55 ml / 2 fl. oz / ¼ cup coconut oil
75 g / 3 oz / ⅓ cup maple syrup
1 tsp vanilla extract
1 medium ripe banana, mashed

Method

1. Preheat the oven to 180°C (160°C fan) / 350F / gas 4. Spray a large baking tray with non-fat cooking spray.

2. Mix together the oats, cinnamon, salt, flaxseed, almonds and raisins in a large bowl.

3. In a small saucepan over medium low heat, warm the coconut oil, maple syrup and vanilla extract. Once melted together, remove from heat and whisk in the mashed banana until well combined.

4. Add to the dry ingredients and mix well to combine. Spread the mixture evenly across the prepared baking tray.

5. Bake for 25–28 minutes or until golden brown. Remove to a wire rack to cool and harden before serving or storing for up to one week in an airtight container.

Fruity Chia Yoghurts

Serves: 4 / Preparation time: 20 minutes
Cooking time: 5 minutes / Calories per portion: 270

Ingredients

2 tbsp chia seeds
300 g / 11 oz / 2 cups raspberries
1 tbsp lemon juice
2 tbsp light agave nectar
225 g / 8 oz / 1 cup coconut milk yoghurt
225 g / 8 oz / 1 cup soya yoghurt
100 g / 3 ½ oz / 1 cup fruit and nut muesli

Method

1. Soak the chia seeds in a bowl of water for 15 minutes.

2. Meanwhile, cook together the raspberries, lemon juice, agave nectar and 2 tbsp of water in a saucepan set over a medium heat.

3. Once the raspberries are soft and juicy, purée in a food processor and pass through a fine sieve into a bowl. Drain the chia seeds when ready and stir into the raspberry purée.

4. Divide the purée between four serving pots. Combine the two yoghurts and spoon into the pots on top of the purée.

5. Top with muesli when ready to serve.

Tropical Oat Porridge

Serves: 4 / Preparation time: 10 minutes

Cooking time: 10 minutes / Calories per portion: 253

Ingredients

85 g / 3 oz / 2 cups rolled oats

350 ml / 12 fl. oz / 1 ½ cups unsweetened almond milk

150 ml / 5 fl. oz / ⅔ cup light coconut milk

a pinch of ground cinnamon

2 tbsp light agave nectar

300 g / 11 oz / 1 ⅓ cups canned pineapple chunks, drained

2 tbsp shelled pistachios, chopped

30 g / 1 oz / ½ cup coconut flakes

Method

1. Combine the oats, both milks, a pinch of ground cinnamon and the agave nectar in a saucepan.

2. Cook over a medium heat, stirring frequently, until thick and creamy.

3. Spoon into bowls and top with the pineapple chunks, pistachios and coconut flakes.

Buckwheat and Spinach Pancakes

Serves: 4 / Preparation time: 10 minutes
Cooking time: 25 minutes / Calories per portion: 288

Ingredients

225 g / 8 oz / 1 ½ cups buckwheat flour

1 ½ tsp gluten-free baking powder

425 ml / 15 fl. oz / 1 ¾ cups unsweetened almond milk

1 tbsp apple cider vinegar

75 ml / 3 fl. oz / ⅓ cup avocado oil

100 g / 3 ½ oz / 2 cups baby spinach, washed

2 large vine tomatoes, sliced

1 tbsp nutritional yeast or grated cheese

salt and freshly ground black pepper

Method

1. Sift the buckwheat flour, baking powder and a pinch of salt into a large mixing bowl. Gradually whisk the almond milk until you have a smooth batter. Stir the apple cider vinegar and 1 tbsp of oil into the batter.

2. Wipe the surface of a crêpe pan with a little oil. Heat over a moderate heat until hot and add a small ladle of batter, letting it run all over the pan, tilting it if necessary.

3. Cook for 1–2 minutes until set and golden and then flip. Cook the other side for a further minute before sliding out of the pan onto a plate. Repeat the method for the remaining pancakes.

4. Heat any remaining avocado oil in the pan and add the spinach and seasoning. Sauté for 2 minutes, stirring occasionally, until wilted. Add the tomatoes and continue to cook until softened.

5. Season to taste and spoon into the pancakes. Fold the edges around the filling and serve on plates with nutritional yeast or cheese to garnish.

Light Bites and Lunches

We often eat lunch in a rush or at our desks, looking for something quick and simple. But quick and simple isn't always best. A sandwich on white bread, with crisps and a fizzy drink, is often a 'meal deal' offer in shops and cafes, but it's one of the worst lunches in terms of nutrition.

It pays to make a bit of effort to get a healthy lunch. Packing your own means that you know exactly what you're getting in terms of ingredients and nutrition and it often tastes better too! It doesn't have to be difficult, either. Smaller portions of dishes you've made for dinner, such as soup or chilli, can make a great packed lunch.

Salads are another good choice for lunch. The fresh vegetables are full of nutrients and taste great!
Just watch out for pre-made salad dressings; they are often high in calories, with a lot of added sugar.

Beetroot Soup

Serves: 4 / Preparation time: 10 minutes

Cooking time: 20 minutes / Calories per portion: 326

Ingredients

2 tbsp avocado oil

1 onion, finely chopped

1 clove of garlic, minced

600 g / 1 lb 5 oz / 4 cups cooked beetroot in juice, drained and chopped

450 g / 1 lb / 4 cups ripe vine tomatoes, halved

500 ml / 18 fl. oz / 2 cups vegetable stock

150 ml / 5 fl. oz / ⅔ cup unsweetened almond milk

4 sprigs of dill, to garnish

4 slices gluten-free bread, to serve

150 g / 5 oz / ⅔ cup soft cheese, to serve

salt and freshly ground black pepper

Method

1. Heat the oil in a large saucepan set over a medium heat until hot. Add the onion, garlic and a pinch of salt, sautéing for 3–4 minutes until translucent.

2. Add the beets, tomatoes, stock and almond milk. Stir well, cook until simmering and continue to cook for a further 10 minutes.

3. Purée the soup in a food processor or blender until mostly smooth whilst retaining a little texture. Return the soup to the saucepan and warm over a low heat, seasoning to taste with salt and pepper.

4. Ladle into serving bowls and serve with a garnish of dill and bread topped with soft cheese on the side.

Rocket, Fig and Walnut Salad

Serves: 4 / Preparation time: 10 minutes
Cooking time: 5 minutes / Calories per portion: 275

Ingredients

75 ml / 3 fl. oz / ⅓ cup avocado oil

3 tbsp balsamic vinegar

½ tsp Dijon mustard

1 tsp dark agave nectar

4 ripe Bursa figs, quartered

225 g / 8 oz / 4 cups rocket (arugula), washed

110 g / 4 oz / 1 cup walnuts, roughly chopped

75 g / 3 oz / ¾ cup firm cheese, cubed

flaked sea salt and freshly ground black pepper

Method

1. Shake together the oil, vinegar, mustard, agave nectar and seasoning in an empty jam jar.

2. Season the figs with salt and pepper.

3. Toss with the rocket, walnuts and cubed cheese in a mixing bowl.

4. Lift into a bowl and serve with the dressing on the side.

Salmon and Vegetable Tart

Serves: 4 / Preparation time: 15 minutes

Cooking time: 45 minutes / Calories per portion: 385

Ingredients

175 g / 6 oz ready-made vegan shortcrust pastry, chilled

gluten-free plain (all-purpose) flour, for dusting

350 g / 12 oz / 3 ⅓ cups firm silken tofu, patted dry

2 tbsp nutritional yeast

3 tbsp hummus

150 g / 5 oz / 1 cup smoked salmon, chopped

1 large leek, thinly sliced, washed and dried

100 g / 3 ½ oz / ⅔ cup cherry tomatoes, halved

110 g / 4 oz / ⅔ cup low-fat feta, crumbled

100 g / 3 ½ oz / 2 cups mixed leaf salad

a few sprigs of thyme, to serve

salt and freshly ground black pepper

Method

1. Preheat the oven to 180°C (160°C) / 350F / gas 4. Roll out the pastry on a lightly floured surface to 1 cm (½ in) thickness. Use the pastry to line the base and sides of a 30 cm x 10 cm x 5 cm (12 in x 4 in x 2 in) fluted tart tin.

2. Prick the base with a fork and chill until ready to use. Combine the tofu, nutritional yeast, hummus and a little seasoning in a food processor. Pulse until the mixture comes together.

3. Scrape into a bowl and add the salmon, leek, cherry tomatoes and stir well. Spoon into the prepared pastry and top with some of the crumbled cheese.

4. Bake for 35–45 minutes until the filling is set and the pastry is golden and cooked through. Remove to a wire rack to cool.

5. Serve the tart with the mixed leaf salad and remaining feta on top.

Butternut and Rocket Pappardelle

Serves: 4 / Preparation time: 10 minutes
Cooking time: 15 minutes / Calories per portion: 386

Ingredients

400 g / 14 oz gluten-free pappardelle
½ butternut squash, peeled and seeded
2 tbsp olive oil
1 clove of garlic, minced
55 g / 2 oz / 1 cup rocket (arugula)
75 g / 3 oz / ½ cup capers in brine, drained
1 lemon, zested and juiced
55 g / 2 oz / 1 cup basil leaves, roughly torn
salt and freshly ground black pepper

Method

1. Cook the pappardelle in a large saucepan of salted, boiling water until 'al dente'; 8–10 minutes.

2. Meanwhile, use a vegetable peeler to peel ribbons from the butternut squash. Heat the oil in a large sauté pan set over a moderate heat until hot.

3. Add the butternut squash and garlic, sautéing for 3–4 minutes until tender. Drain the pappardelle when ready and add it to the squash along with half a cup of the cooking liquid, tossing well to coat.

4. Add the rocket and capers, toss well and adjust to taste using lemon juice, lemon zest, salt and pepper.

5. Lift the pasta into serving plates and serve with torn basil on top.

Kale and Bean Soup

Serves: 4 / Preparation time: 10 minutes
Cooking time: 45 minutes / Calories per portion: 378

Ingredients

3 tbsp avocado oil

1 onion, finely chopped

2 carrots, peeled and finely diced

2 sticks of celery, finely diced

1 bouquet garni

400 g / 14 oz / 2 cups passata

400 g / 14 oz / 2 cups canned cannellini beans, drained

1 l / 1 pint 16 fl. oz / 4 cups low-sodium vegetable stock

140 g / 5 oz / 2 cups curly kale, chopped

gluten-free bread, to serve

110 g / 4 oz / 1 cup low-fat cheese, grated

salt and freshly ground black pepper

Method

1. Heat the oil in a large saucepan set over a moderate heat until hot. Add the onion, carrot, celery, bouquet garni and salt.

2. Cook for 4 minutes, stirring occasionally, until softened and translucent. Cover with the passata, beans and stock, stirring well.

3. Cook until simmering, then reduce the heat to low and continue to cook for a further 25–30 minutes until the beans are tender.

4. Once the beans are tender, stir in the kale and cook for a further 5 minutes until tender. Adjust the seasoning to taste.

5. Heat the grill to hot. Top slices of bread with a little cheese and seasoning. Grill for a minute until the cheese is melted. Serve the crostini alongside bowls of the soup.

Ceviche with Avocado

Serves: 4 / Preparation time: 10 minutes + chilling
Cooking time: 25 minutes / Calories per portion: 299

Ingredients

3 lemons

½ tsp light agave nectar

2 vine tomatoes, cored and diced

1 pink grapefruit, peeled and segmented

1 small red onion, finely chopped

2 red chillies (chilies), finely chopped

450 g / 1 lb turbot fillet, skinned and
  pin-boned

1 large ripe avocado, pitted and sliced

salt and freshly ground black pepper

Method

1. Juice two lemons into a bowl. Cut the third
   into wedges and reserve as a garnish.

2. Add the agave nectar, tomato, grapefruit,
   red onion, chilli and seasoning to the lemon
   juice, whisking well to incorporate.

3. Thinly slice the turbot fillet and arrange on
   a serving platter. Pour over the some of the
   lemon dressing.

4. Add the avocado and pour over the
   remaining dressing. Cover and chill for
   15 minutes.

5. When ready, serve the ceviche fresh from
   the fridge.

Tomato and Aubergine Galette

Serves: 4 / Preparation time: 15 minutes
Cooking time: 50 minutes / Calories per portion: 275

Ingredients

150 g / 5 oz ready-made vegan shortcrust pastry

a little gluten-free plain (all-purpose) flour, for dusting

1 large aubergine (eggplant), cut into 1 cm (½ in) slices

75 ml / 3 fl. oz / ⅓ cup avocado oil

2 large vine tomatoes, cored and sliced

½ tsp dried basil

2 tbsp unsweetened almond milk

a few sprigs of basil, to garnish

flaked sea salt and freshly ground black pepper

Method

1. Preheat the oven to 180°C (160°C fan) / 350F / gas 4.

2. Roll out the pastry on a lightly floured surface into a round approximately 30 cm (12 in) in diameter and 1 cm (½ in) thick. Lift the round of pastry onto a large round baking tray.

3. Preheat a griddle pan over a moderate heat until hot. Brush both sides of the aubergine with oil and season generously.

4. Griddle in the hot pan for 2 minutes on both sides until lightly charred. Remove from the pan and pat dry. Arrange the sliced aubergine and tomato, overlapping, in the centre of the pastry, leaving a 2 cm (1 in) border all the way around.

5. Sprinkle the dried basil over the vegetables and then fold the border of the pastry back over and brush the exposed top with almond milk.

6. Bake for 30–40 minutes until the pastry is golden and cooked. Remove to a wire rack and serve with a garnish of basil.

Courgette Farfalle

Serves: 4 / Preparation time: 10 minutes
Cooking time: 10 minutes / Calories per portion: 371

Ingredients

300 g / 11 oz / 4 cups gluten-free farfalle

2 small courgettes (zucchinis)

2 tbsp avocado oil

1 clove of garlic, minced

½ lemon, juiced

1 tbsp nutritional yeast

a small bunch of thyme sprigs

a pinch of saffron threads

salt and freshly ground black pepper

Method

1. Cook the pasta in a large saucepan of salted, boiling water until 'al dente'; 8–10 minutes.

2. Meanwhile, prepare the courgette by peeling into thin strips using a vegetable peeler. Heat the oil in a large sauté pan set over a medium heat until hot.

3. Add the garlic and fry for 30 seconds. Add the courgette and continue to fry for a further 3–4 minutes until softened.

4. Drain the pasta, reserving half a cup of the cooking liquid and add to the courgette. Toss well, loosening with a little of the cooking liquid as necessary.

5. Season to taste with salt and pepper. Spoon the pasta into bowls and garnish with the yeast, thyme and a pinch of saffron threads on top.

Main Meals

If you've stuck to your calorie goals at breakfast and lunch and avoided snacking, it can be tempting to treat yourself and overindulge at dinner. For most of us, dinner is the main meal of the day, so it's important to make it count. You won't have to make many changes to make an average meal extraordinarily healthy.

It's good to get a hit of protein in your main meal, but some proteins are better than others. Stick to fish or lean meat and avoid fatty meats or those with the skin still on. And don't forget that pulses, nuts and beans provide protein too! Steaming and grilling meat are healthier options than frying in oil.

Swap out bread rolls, white rice or plain pasta for wholegrain versions, or go for a jacket potato instead. Fill the rest of your plate with fresh vegetables, such as steamed broccoli or French beans, roasted tomatoes or a salad of spinach leaves and bell peppers.

Fruity Couscous Salad

Serves: 4 / Preparation time: 30 minutes
Calories per portion: 388

Ingredients

225 g / 8 oz / 1⅓ cups couscous

600 ml / 1 pint 2 fl. oz / 2 ½ cups low-sodium vegetable stock

140 g / 5 oz / 3 cups baby spinach, washed

6 medjool dates, pitted and sliced

110 g / 4 oz / ¾ cup pomegranate seeds

55 g / 2 oz / ⅓ cup raisins

2 tbsp shelled pistachios

1 lemon, juiced

salt and freshly ground black pepper

Method

1. Place the couscous in a heatproof bowl. Add the stock, stir once and cover the bowl with cling film or a plate.

2. Set the couscous to one side for 10–15 minutes until it has absorbed the stock. Fluff with a fork and stir in the spinach. Cover again and leave the spinach to wilt for 5 minutes.

3. Stir in the remaining ingredients and season to taste with salt and pepper before serving.

Potato and Avocado Burger

Serves: 4 / Preparation time: 15 minutes
Cooking time: 40 minutes / Calories per portion: 431

Ingredients

1.2 kg / 2 lb 10 oz / 8 cups floury potatoes, peeled and diced

2 tbsp Dijon mustard

110 g / 4 oz / ½ cup coconut milk yoghurt

½ clove of garlic, minced

1 tbsp lemon juice

1 tbsp coconut oil

1 ½ tbsp cornflour (cornstarch), plus extra for dusting

3 tbsp avocado oil

2 small ripe avocados, pitted and sliced

55 g / 2 oz / 1 cup rocket (arugula), washed

salt and freshly ground black pepper

Method

1. Cook the potatoes in a large saucepan of salted, boiling water for 15–20 minutes until tender to the point of a knife.

2. Meanwhile, whisk together the mustard, yoghurt, garlic, lemon juice and a little seasoning to make a quick sauce. Cover and chill.

3. Drain the potatoes and leave to steam dry briefly before mashing with the coconut oil, cornflour and seasoning until smooth.

4. Shape the mixture into 12 small patties and dust with cornflour, shaking off the excess. Season with salt and pepper and heat the avocado oil in a sauté pan set over a moderate heat until hot.

5. Fry the patties for 2–3 minutes on both sides, working in batches, until golden and crisp. Brush the avocado with a little sauce and stack with the rocket between patties.

Pulled Pork with Guacamole

Serves: 4 / Preparation time: 10 minutes

Cooking time: 2 hours 10 minutes / Calories per portion: 390

Ingredients

2 tbsp avocado oil

4 cloves of garlic, minced

1 tbsp taco seasoning

2 tbsp dark agave nectar

100 ml / 3 ½ fl. oz / ½ cup apple cider vinegar

600 ml / 1 pint 2 fl. oz / 2 ½ cups chicken stock

750 g / 1 lb 10 oz pork tenderloin, trimmed and scored

2 limes

1 large ripe avocado, pitted and chopped

1 red onion

a bunch of coriander (cilantro)

1 head of lettuce, leaves separated

salt and freshly ground black pepper

Method

1. Heat the oil in a large casserole dish set over a moderate heat until hot. Add three cloves of minced garlic and fry for 1 minute.

2. Add the taco seasoning, stir well and cook for a further minute. Add the agave, vinegar and chicken stock.

3. Cook until simmering, stirring occasionally, and add the pork. Cover with a lid and cook on a low heat for 2 hours until the pork breaks apart.

4. Remove the pork from the sauce and pat dry. Shred between two forks and stir back into the sauce, seasoning with salt and pepper.

5. Juice one lime into a bowl and add the remaining garlic and the avocado. Finely chop half the onion and some coriander, adding it to the bowl. Mash everything until smooth and season to taste.

6. Cut the remaining lime into wedges and thinly slice the remaining onion. Serve the pork on lettuce leaves with guacamole, red onion and lime wedges to garnish.

Oriental Vegetable Noodles

Serves: 4 / Preparation time: 10 minutes

Cooking time: 10 minutes / Calories per portion: 282

Ingredients

2 tbsp sesame oil

1 clove of garlic, minced

1 small knob of ginger, peeled and grated

2 medium courgettes (zucchini), seeded and cut into long strips

2 medium carrots, peeled and julienned

400 g / 14 oz cooked wholegrain noodles

3 tbsp dark soy sauce

2 tbsp rice wine vinegar

1 tbsp sesame seeds

freshly ground black pepper

a small handful of Thai basil leaves

Method

1. Heat the oil in a wok or large sauté pan set over a moderate heat until hot.

2. Add the garlic, ginger, courgette and carrot, sautéing for 3–4 minutes.

3. Add the noodles, soy sauce, vinegar, sesame seeds and a few basil leaves. Toss well and cook for a further 2–3 minutes until the noodles are warmed through. Season with black pepper.

4. Lift into bowls and serve with a garnish of basil leaves on top.

Pumpkin and Ham Risotto

Serves: 4 / Preparation time: 10 minutes
Cooking time: 45 minutes / Calories per portion: 385

Ingredients

2 tbsp olive oil

2 cloves of garlic, minced

2 shallots, finely chopped

1 carrot, finely diced

75 g / 3 oz / ½ cup ham, chopped

200 g / 7 oz / 1 ½ cups Arborio rice

2 tbsp white wine vinegar

1000 ml / 1 pint 16 fl. oz / 4 cups low-sodium
   vegetable stock

225 g / 8 oz / 1 cup canned unsweetened
   pumpkin purée

110 g / 4 oz / ½ cup coconut milk yoghurt

a small handful of sage leaves, to garnish

salt and freshly ground black pepper

Method

1. Heat the oil in a large saucepan set over
   a medium heat until hot. Add the garlic,
   shallot, carrot and a little seasoning,
   sweating them for 4–5 minutes.

2. Stir in the ham and rice and cook for a
   further 3–4 minutes until the grains start to
   turn translucent. Deglaze the pan with the
   white wine vinegar and 2 tbsp of water
   and then reduce the heat slightly.

3. Add a ladle of stock to the rice, stirring
   and cooking until absorbed, before adding
   another. Keep adding the stock, one ladle
   at a time, for 25–35 minutes until the rice
   has absorbed all the stock and is creamy
   and tender.

4. Stir in the pumpkin purée and season the
   risotto to taste. Spoon onto plates and top
   with the yoghurt, sage leaves and a little
   more seasoning when ready to serve.

Sausage and Kale Stew

Serves: 4 / Preparation time: 15 minutes
Cooking time: 35 minutes / Calories per portion: 437

Ingredients

2 tbsp olive oil

1 large onion, finely chopped

2 cloves of garlic, minced

300 g / 11 oz smoked sausage, roughly chopped

450 g / 1 lb / 3 cups Maris Piper potatoes, peeled and diced

1.25 l / 2 pints 4 fl. oz / 5 cups low-sodium vegetable stock

200 g / 7 oz / 3 cups curly kale, chopped

a small bunch of flat-leaf parsley, chopped

salt and freshly ground black pepper

Method

1. Heat the oil in a large casserole dish set over a medium heat until hot. Add the onion, garlic and a little salt, sweating for 3–4 minutes until softened.

2. Add the sausage and potato, cooking for a further 3–4 minutes. Pour in the stock, stir well and cook until simmering.

3. Once simmering, reduce the heat slightly and cook for a further 20 minutes or until the potato is tender.

4. Once tender, stir in the kale and continue to cook for a further 5 minutes until softened. Stir through the parsley and adjust the seasoning to taste.

5. Ladle into bowls and serve immediately.

Green Tea Baked Tofu

Serves: 4 / Preparation time: 15 minutes
Cooking time: 20 minutes / Calories per portion: 389

Ingredients

600 g / 1 lb 5 oz firm tofu

100 g / 3 ½ oz / ⅔ cup silken tofu

1 tbsp coconut oil

110 g / 4 oz / 2 ½ cups panko breadcrumbs, crushed

250 ml / 9 fl. oz / 1 cup green tea

2 tbsp soy sauce

1 tsp dark agave nectar

1 tbsp arrowroot powder, mixed with 1 tbsp warm water

55 g / 2 oz / ½ cup walnuts, chopped

1 head of iceberg lettuce

4 salad tomatoes, cut into decorative garnishes

salt and freshly ground black pepper

Method

1. Preheat the oven to 230°C (210°C fan) / 450F / gas 9. Line a baking tray with greaseproof paper.

2. Cut the firm tofu into squares and pat dry. Purée the silken tofu and coconut oil with 1 tbsp of warm water in a food processor until smooth.

3. Dip the squares of tofu in the silken tofu mixture, shaking off any excess. Coat in the crushed panko and season with salt and pepper. Arrange on the baking tray.

4. Bake for 10–12 minutes until golden and crisp. Meanwhile, combine the green tea, soy sauce and agave nectar in a saucepan.

5. Warm over a moderate heat and then cook until boiling. Whisk in enough arrowroot paste to thicken the sauce. Stir in the walnuts and set to one side.

6. Remove the crispy tofu to a wire rack. Dress serving plates with lettuce leaves and the tomatoes. Top with the tofu and the sauce before serving.

Lamb Chops with Tomato Salsa

Serves: 4 / Preparation time: 10 minutes
Cooking time: 20 minutes / Calories per portion: 453

Ingredients

4 bone-in lamb chops, trimmed

75 ml / 3 fl. oz / ⅓ cup avocado oil

1 aubergine (eggplant), split in half

2 tbsp balsamic vinegar

1 lime, juiced

1 tsp agave nectar

450 g / 1 lb / 3 cups vine tomatoes, cored, seeded and diced

1 small red onion, finely chopped

1 clove of garlic, minced

1 small bunch of coriander (cilantro), roughly chopped

150 g / 5 oz / 1 ½ cups asparagus, woody ends removed

salt and freshly ground black pepper

Method

1. Preheat the oven to 200°C (180°C fan) / 400F / gas 6. Rub the lamb chops with oil and season. Arrange in a roasting tray and brush the aubergine with balsamic vinegar. Season and position alongside the chops.

2. Roast for 15 minutes or until the lamb registers at least 66°C / 150F on a meat thermometer.

3. Meanwhile, stir together the remaining oil with the lime juice, agave nectar and seasoning in a mixing bowl. Add the tomato, red onion, garlic and chopped coriander and stir well. Cover and set to one side.

4. Remove the chops from the oven once ready and leave to rest, covered loosely, for 5 minutes. Return the aubergine to the oven for a further 3 minutes.

5. Cook the asparagus in a large saucepan of salted, boiling water for 2 minutes until tender. Drain well and season to taste.

6. Serve the chops on plates with the salsa, roast aubergine and asparagus on the side.

Desserts

You may think that trying to lose weight means giving up desserts entirely, but it doesn't have to be that way. Planning one or two into your menu for the week can be a great incentive for sticking to your targets. Even desserts can be low-calorie if you choose the right ones!

Some desserts use the natural sweetness of fruit or the richer texture of nuts to deliver nutrients in a tasty package. These ingredients can make some puddings healthier, too. Why not make a simple fruit crumble? Instead of using plain flour and white sugar in the topping, use a mixture of ground almonds and oats with a smaller amount of coconut sugar, or use powdered stevia instead.

Portion control is just as important with desserts as it is with other meals. Use a small plate or bowl and be firm about sticking to a single helping. One of the best desserts you can choose isn't food at all. Instead, take a brisk walk as your last 'course'.

Pomegranate Frozen Yoghurt

Serves: 4 / Preparation time: 10 minutes + freezing
Cooking time: 10 minutes / Calories per portion: 299

Ingredients

450 g / 1 lb / 2 cups coconut milk yoghurt
450 g / 1 lb / 2 cups soy milk yoghurt
55 g / 2 oz / ¼ cup light agave nectar
140 g / 5 oz / 1 cup raspberries
110 g / 4 oz / 1 cup pomegranate seeds
2 tbsp shelled pistachios, chopped

Method

1. Mix together the coconut and soy milk yoghurt with 2 tbsp of the agave nectar. Pour into a ice cream maker and churn until softly frozen.

2. Scrape into a freezable container and freeze for 4 hours.

3. Combine the remaining agave nectar with the raspberries, most of the pomegranate seeds and 2 tbsp of water in a saucepan. Cook over a low heat until the fruit is very soft.

4. Purée with a stick blender until smooth. Stir in the remaining pomegranate seeds.

5. When the frozen yoghurt is ready to serve, scoop into dishes and top with the sauce and pistachios.

Coconut Cake

Serves: 12 / Preparation time: 20 minutes
Cooking time: 35 minutes / Calories per portion: 317

Ingredients

700 ml / 1 pint 5 fl. oz / 3 cups unsweetened almond milk

1 tbsp ground flaxseed

1 tbsp apple cider vinegar

225 g / 8 oz / 1 ½ cups gluten-free plain (all-purpose) flour

150 g / 5 oz / 1 cup coconut flour

3 tsp gluten-free baking powder

1 ½ tsp bicarbonate of (baking) soda

225 g / 8 oz / 1 cup coconut sugar

55 ml / 2 fl. oz / ¼ cup coconut oil, melted

300 g / 11 oz / 1 ⅓ cups coconut milk yoghurt

2 tsp vanilla extract

2 tbsp light agave nectar

120 g / 4 oz / 1 ½ cups coconut flesh, shredded

Method

1. Preheat the oven to 180°C (160°C fan) / 350F / gas 4. Grease and line a 20 cm (8 in) round springform cake tin with greaseproof paper.

2. Whisk together the almond milk, flaxseed and vinegar in a bowl. Leave to one side for at least 5 minutes.

3. Meanwhile, sift together the flours, baking powder and bicarbonate of soda into a large mixing bowl. Add the coconut sugar and coconut oil to the bowl with the almond milk, stirring well.

4. Pour the wet ingredients into the dry and stir well until you have a smooth batter. Scrape the mixture into the prepared tin and level the batter if needed.

5. Bake for 25–35 minutes until golden and risen and the cake tester comes out clean. Remove to a wire rack to cool.

6. Beat together the coconut yoghurt, vanilla extract and agave nectar until smooth. Turn out the cake, top with the yoghurt and grate over fresh coconut to serve.

Coconut Milk Panna Cotta

Serves: 4 / Preparation time: 15 minutes + chilling
Cooking time: 10 minutes / Calories per portion: 330

Ingredients

300 g / 11 oz / 2 cups strawberries, hulled and halved

½ lemon, juiced

2 tbsp light agave nectar

3 tsp agar agar powder, dissolved in 100 ml / 3 ½ fl. oz / ½ cup warm water

3 tsp tapioca flour

600 ml / 1 pint 2 fl. oz / 2 ½ cups light coconut milk

110 g / 4 oz / ½ cup coconut sugar

Method

1. Combine the strawberries with the lemon juice, agave nectar and 2 tbsp of water in a saucepan. Cook over a medium heat until the fruit is soft and juicy.

2. Purée the mixture until smooth and then pass through a fine sieve into a jar. Leave to cool and then chill.

3. Blend the agar agar mixture in a food processor for 3 minutes. Add the tapioca flour and blend for a further minute.

4. Combine the coconut milk and coconut sugar in a large saucepan set over a medium heat. Cook, stirring frequently, until the sugar has dissolved. Add the agar agar mixture and bring to a simmer for 1 minute.

5. Pour everything back into the food processor and blend until smooth. Strain the mixture into a jug and divide between four serving glasses.

6. Let the mixture cool for 5 minutes and then cover and chill for 4 hours until set. Serve with the strawberry sauce on top.

Apple Sorbet Tartlets

Serves: 6 / Preparation time: 20 minutes + freezing

Cooking time: 1 hour 10 minutes / Calories per portion: 411

Ingredients

500 ml / 18 fl. oz / 2 cups apple juice

600 g / 1 lb 5 oz / 4 cups Gala apples, cored and quartered

100 g / 3 ½ oz / ½ cup dark agave nectar

¾ tsp ground cinnamon, plus extra to garnish

2 tbsp apple brandy

150 g / 5 oz / 1 cup gluten-free plain (all-purpose) flour, sifted

100 g / 3 ½ oz / 1 cup ground almonds

½ tsp gluten-free baking powder

75 g / 3 oz / ½ cup coconut sugar

75 ml / 3 fl. oz / ⅓ cup coconut oil, melted

1 large ripe banana, mashed

a few sprigs of mint, to garnish

Method

1. Preheat the oven to 180°C (160°C fan) / 350F / gas 4. Combine the apple juice, apples, agave nectar and cinnamon in a baking dish, covering it with foil. Bake for 40–45 minutes until the fruit is soft. Purée everything in a food processor until smooth and then pass through a sieve into a bowl.

2. Stir through the apple brandy and then churn in an ice cream maker. Once the sorbet is soft and frozen, scrape into a freezable container. Freeze for 4 hours.

3. Combine the flour, ground almonds, baking powder and coconut sugar in a mixing bowl. Whisk together the coconut oil, 75 ml / 3 fl. oz / ⅓ cup warm water and the banana in a mixing jug.

4. Add the wet ingredients to the dry and mix well. Press into six mini tartlet cases and arrange on a baking tray. Bake for 22–25 minutes until golden and firm. Remove to a wire rack to cool.

5. Position the sorbet in the baskets. Garnish with cinnamon and mint.

Almond and Blueberry Creams

Serves: 4 / Preparation time: 15 minutes + chilling
Cooking time: 5 minutes / Calories per portion: 243

Ingredients

55 g / 2 oz / ½ cup almonds

600 ml / 1 pint 2 fl. oz / 2 ½ cups
unsweetened almond milk

2 tsp agar agar powder

2 tsp tapioca flour

75 g / 2 ½ oz / ⅓ cup light agave nectar

110 g / 4 oz / ½ cup coconut milk yoghurt

150 g / 5 oz / 1 cup blueberries

Method

1. Soak the almonds in the almond milk for
   1 hour. Blend the mixture in a food
   processor until smooth.

2. Warm the almond liquid in a saucepan
   set over a medium heat. Once simmering,
   combine with the agar agar powder in
   a food processor. Blend on high for
   3 minutes.

3. Add the tapioca flour, agave nectar and
   coconut yoghurt, blending for a further
   2 minutes. Add the blueberries and pulse
   a few times.

4. Divide the mixture between serving pots.
   Cover and chill for 4 hours until ready
   to serve.

Cheesecake Bites

Serves: 8 / Preparation time: 25 minutes + soaking and chilling
Calories per portion: 412

Ingredients

225 g / 8 oz / 1 ½ cups cashews
150 g / 5 oz / 1 cup pitted dates
165 g / 6 oz / 1 ½ cups walnuts
1 lemon, juiced
75 ml / 3 fl. oz / ⅓ cup coconut oil, melted
150 ml / 5 fl. oz / ⅔ cup coconut milk
110 g / 4 oz / ½ cup light agave nectar

Method

1. Soak the cashews in a bowl of boiling water for 1 hour. After 50 minutes, soak the dates in hot water for 15 minutes. Drain the dates and process in a food processor until they form into a ball.

2. Remove the dates and add 110 g / 4 oz / 1 cup of the walnuts, blending until mealy. Return the processed dates and pulse until a rough dough forms. Press into the base of an 18 cm (7 in) square baking tin lined with greaseproof paper. Chill until ready.

3. Drain the cashews and add to the food processor along with the lemon juice, coconut oil, coconut milk and agave nectar. Blend on high until smooth.

4. Pour on top of the chilled base. Chop the remaining walnuts and scatter on top, pressing them into the filling.

5. Cover and freeze for 4 hours until set and firm. Remove from the freezer and leave to stand at room temperature for 10 minutes before cutting and serving.

Coconut and Mint Tart

Serves: 8 / Preparation time: 25 minutes + chilling
Cooking time: 20 minutes / Calories per portion: 379

Ingredients

150 g / 5 oz / 1 cup gluten-free plain
  (all-purpose) flour, plus extra for dusting
100 g / 3 ½ oz / ⅔ cup buckwheat flour
100 ml / 3 ½ fl. oz / ½ cup coconut oil
110 ml / 4 fl. oz / ½ cup water
300 g / 11 oz / 2 cups peas
100 g / 3 ½ oz / ½ cup light agave nectar
2 tbsp mint leaves, plus extra to garnish
125 ml / 4 ½ fl. oz / ½ cup light coconut milk
450 g / 1 lb / 2 cups coconut milk yoghurt
2 tbsp pistachios

Method

1. Combine the flours and salt in a mixing
   bowl. Add 3 tbsp of oil and incorporate
   with a fork. Add the water, mixing until
   absorbed, then knead lightly until the
   dough comes together into a ball.

2. Turn out the dough onto a lightly floured
   surface and roll it out into a round to fit
   a 20 cm (8 in) fluted tin. Press the dough
   gently into the base and sides of the tin.
   Prick the base with a fork and line with
   greaseproof paper and baking beans.
   Chill for 15 minutes.

3. Preheat the oven to 180°C (160°C fan) /
   350°F / gas 4. Blind-bake the pastry for
   15 minutes. Discard the beans and paper
   and return to the oven for 5 minutes.
   Remove to a wire rack to cool.

4. Blend the peas with the remaining oil,
   agave nectar, mint leaves, coconut milk
   and coconut yoghurt in food processor
   until smooth. Spread the filling into the
   pastry and garnish with pistachios and
   mint leaves before serving.

Chocolate Mousse

Serves: 4 / Preparation time: 15 minutes + chilling
Cooking time: 5 minutes / Calories per portion: 401

Ingredients

400 g / 14 oz can of coconut milk, chilled overnight

1 tsp vanilla extract

150 g / 5 oz / 1 cup dairy-free dark chocolate, chopped

1 orange

140 g / 5 oz / 1 cup raspberries, to serve

Method

1. Carefully open the can of coconut milk and spoon the thick cream into a mixing bowl, discarding the water.

2. Beat with the vanilla extract until thick. Meanwhile, melt the chocolate in a heatproof bowl set atop a half-filled saucepan of simmering water, stirring occasionally.

3. Beat the melted chocolate into the coconut cream and then divide the mixture between four serving ramekins.

4. Cover and chill for 2 hours.

5. When ready to serve, grate over fresh orange zest and serve with raspberries.

Healthy Snacks

Snacking can be one of the biggest pitfalls when trying to lose weight. You're eating smaller meals, which often means you end up craving snacks. Unfortunately, some of the most convenient and appealing snacks are loaded with sugar and other unhealthy ingredients.

There is good news, though! When you change your diet in favour of nutrient-rich food, it means that you feel full for longer, and the slow-burning energy keeps you going until the next meal. Once you get into it, you'll find that you don't crave snacks as much.

Even so, there's no harm in keeping your energy up with a healthy snack here and there. A handful of nuts or seeds provides protein and energy, so keep them handy in your bag or desk drawer. Veggies dipped in hummus are another good choice and so is a piece of fresh fruit.

Salmon and Polenta Skewers

Serves: 4 / Preparation time: 10 minutes
Cooking time: 10 minutes / Calories per portion: 341

Ingredients

450 g / 1 lb / 4 cups salmon fillet, cubed

300 g / 11 oz firm cooked polenta, cubed

30 g / 1 oz / 1 cup dried wakame seaweed, torn

3 tbsp avocado oil

4 wooden skewers, soaked in water for 30 minutes

30 g / 1 oz / ½ cup rocket (arugula)

30 g / 1 oz / 1 cup beansprouts

salt and freshly ground black pepper

Method

1. Preheat the grill to hot.

2. Thread the salmon, polenta and seaweed onto the skewers, alternating as necessary. Brush with oil and season with salt and pepper.

3. Arrange on a grilling tray; grill for 6–8 minutes until the polenta is golden and the salmon is firm to the touch and pink.

4. Serve with rocket and beansprouts as a garnish.

Spinach Quesadillas

Serves: 4 / Preparation time: 10 minutes

Cooking time: 15 minutes / Calories per portion: 312

Ingredients

non-fat cooking spray

4 large gluten-free tortilla wraps

225 g / 8 oz / 2 cups dairy-free firm
  cheese, grated

150 g / 5 oz / 3 cups baby spinach, washed

salt and freshly ground black pepper

Method

1. Coat a large sauté pan with non-fat
   cooking spray. Heat over a medium heat
   and lay a tortilla down in the pan.

2. Top with half of the cheese and the
   spinach. Season with salt and pepper
   and top with another tortilla, pressing
   down with a spatula.

3. Cook for 3–4 minutes until golden
   underneath. Flip the quesadilla and press
   down with the spatula, cooking for a further
   2–3 minutes until golden underneath.

4. Repeat with the remaining tortillas, cheese
   and spinach to make another quesadilla.

5. Cut the quesadillas into slices and serve.

Salmon Maki Rolls

Serves: 4 / Preparation time: 25 minutes
Calories per portion: 228

Ingredients

450 g / 1 lb skinless salmon fillet, pin-boned
2 tbsp light soy sauce
2 large nori sheets
150 g / 5 oz / 1 cup cooked sushi rice, cold
55 ml / 2 fl. oz / ¼ cup rice wine vinegar
a small handful of cress, to garnish

Method

1. Slice the salmon lengthwise into thin strips. Season with soy sauce and chill until needed.

2. Line a sushi mat with cling film. Lay a sheet of nori down and top with half the cooked sushi rice. Season the rice with some rice wine vinegar.

3. Top with half the sliced salmon and then use the sushi mat to help you roll the sushi. Chill as you prepare the other roll in the same fashion with the remaining ingredients.

4. Using a sharp knife cut the rolls into pieces and serve with a garnish of cress on top.

Tomato Gratins

Serves: 8 / Preparation time: 15 minutes
Cooking time: 10 minutes / Calories per portion: 197

Ingredients

1 tbsp coriander seeds

1 tsp cumin seeds

1 tsp black peppercorns

8 mini gluten-free tortillas

2 tbsp olive oil

225 g / 8 oz / 1 cup mozarella, cubed

4 Roma tomatoes, sliced

2 spring onions (scallions), sliced

225 g / 8 oz / 1 ½ cups tomatillos, diced

1 lime, juiced

1 tbsp distilled vinegar

a few sprigs of coriander (cilantro), to garnish

flaked sea salt

Method

1. Preheat the grill to hot. Toast the spices in a dry frying pan set over a moderate heat until hot.

2. Coarsely grind in a mortar and pestle or spice grinder, seasoning with salt. Brush the tortillas with olive oil and grill for a minute on both sides.

3. Remove from the grill and top with the cheese and slices of tomato. Season with the spice mix and return the gratin to the grill for 1–2 minutes until the mozarella is melted and the tomatoes browned.

4. Toss the spring onions and tomatillo with the lime juice, vinegar and seasoning. Spoon on top of the gratins and serve with a garnish of coriander.

Chicken Skewers

Serves: 4 / Preparation time: 25 minutes
Cooking time: 15 minutes / Calories per portion: 215

Ingredients

1 tsp cumin seeds

1 tsp coriander seeds

1 tbsp white sesame seeds

2 tbsp avocado oil

2 tbsp rice wine vinegar

2 tbsp tamari soy sauce

4 small skinless chicken breasts, cut into 8 strips

75 g / 3 oz / 1 ½ cups rocket (arugula)

110 g / 4 oz / ½ cup unsweetened tomato sauce

8 bamboo skewers, soaked in water for 30 minutes

Method

1. Toast the spices and sesame seeds in a dry frying pan set over a moderate heat until hot.

2. Once the spices are fragrant, grind in a mortar and pestle or in a spice grinder. Combine with the avocado oil, vinegar and soy sauce in a small bowl.

3. Coat the chicken strips in the marinade and leave for 15 minutes.

4. Preheat the grill to hot. Thread the chicken onto the skewers and grill for 8–10 minutes, turning occasionally, until golden and cooked through.

5. Serve on a bed of rocket with tomato sauce for dipping.

Pumpkin Seed Dip

Serves: 4 / Preparation time: 10 minutes
Calories per portion: 403

Ingredients

a large handful of basil leaves, plus extra
    to garnish

110 g / 4 oz / ⅔ cup pumpkin seeds

55 g / 2 oz / ⅓ cup green olives, pitted

75 ml / 3 fl. oz / ⅓ cup avocado oil

55 ml / 2 fl. oz / ¼ cup warm water

1 lime, juiced

2 tbsp nutritional yeast

gluten-free pitta bread, to serve

Method

1. Combine the basil leaves, pumpkin seeds
   (reserving a tablespoon for garnish) and
   olives in a food processor.

2. Pulse until the mixture starts to come
   together. Slowly add the oil, warm water
   and enough lime juice while blending to
   bring the dip together.

3. Stir the nutritional yeast into the dip and
   season it to taste. Serve garnished with the
   reserved seeds, some pitta bread and
   a garnish of basil leaves.

Zesty Cauliflower Salad

Serves: 4 / Preparation time: 15 minutes
Cooking time: 5 minutes / Calories per portion: 95

Ingredients

2 small heads of cauliflower, prepared
  into florets

2 lemons

2 tbsp avocado oil

½ clove of garlic, crushed

a small bunch of chives, snipped

salt and freshly ground black pepper

Method

1. Cook the cauliflower in a large saucepan of salted, boiling water for 4–5 minutes until tender to the point of a knife.

2. Drain well and refresh immediately in iced water.

3. Pare the zest from the lemons and julienne with a sharp knife. Halve and juice the lemons into a bowl and add the avocado oil, garlic and seasoning, whisking well.

4. Drain the cauliflower, pay dry and season generously. Toss in the lemon dressing and spoon into dishes.

5. Top with a garnish of chives and lemon zest before serving.

Raw Superfood Bar

Makes: 8 / Preparation time: 20 minutes + chilling
Calories per portion: 222

Ingredients

225 g / 8 oz / 1 ½ cups dates, pitted
100 g / 3 ½ oz / ⅓ cup dried cranberries
85 g / 3 oz / 2 cups rolled oats
55 g / 2 oz / ⅓ cup golden raisins
55 g / 2 oz / ½ cup pistachios, shelled
2 tbsp golden flaxseed
1 banana, mashed

Method

1. Soak the dates and cranberries in a bowl of hot water for 10 minutes. Meanwhile, grease and line a small shallow baking tray with greaseproof paper.

2. Drain the fruit and blend in a food processor with the oats, raisins, pistachios, flaxseeds and banana. Add a little hot water if the mixture is too stiff.

3. Spoon the mixture into the lined baking tray and flatten out. Cover and chill for 1 hour or until firm.

4. Turn out and cut into bars before serving.

Meal Plan and Diary

Whenever you start a new project, it's important to have a plan and changing your diet is no different! Without a plan, you're likely to have a day where you're pressed for time and don't have a good variety of healthy ingredients. When that happens, you may reach for whatever is available or order a takeaway and fall right off the wagon.

Before you start, sit down and think about how you want to tackle changing your diet. After all, everyone is different. Do you think you have the willpower to go cold turkey or will it work better to cut out those guilty pleasures more gradually? Jot down some targets for exercise and weight loss and be realistic about how fast you think you can drop the pounds. Losing weight gradually is healthier and you're more likely to keep it off than if you follow a crash diet.

It also helps to make a list of what you hope to achieve by changing your diet. Better overall health, clearer skin, more energy – there are a lot of benefits to a healthy diet! Having a list posted where you can see it will help keep you focused on your goals.

In this chapter, you can plan and track your progress for four weeks. When planning your meals, you can mix and match the recipes in this book, or search out your own. The internet is full of help and advice for healthy eating. Once you get into the swing of things, it will become second nature!

Week 1

	Breakfast	Lunch	Snack	Dinner
Monday				
Tuesday				
Wednesday				
Thursday				
Friday				
Saturday				
Sunday				

Starting weight

Finishing weight

Exercise log

New foods that I've tried

How I feel

Week 2

	Breakfast	Lunch	Snack	Dinner
Monday				
Tuesday				
Wednesday				
Thursday				
Friday				
Saturday				
Sunday				

Starting weight

Finishing weight

Exercise log

New foods that I've tried

How I feel

Week 3

	Breakfast	Lunch	Snack	Dinner
Monday				
Tuesday				
Wednesday				
Thursday				
Friday				
Saturday				
Sunday				

Starting weight

Finishing weight

Exercise log

New foods that I've tried

How I feel

Week 4

	Breakfast	Lunch	Snack	Dinner
Monday				
Tuesday				
Wednesday				
Thursday				
Friday				
Saturday				
Sunday				

Starting weight

Finishing weight

Exercise log

New foods that I've tried

How I feel

Shopping List

It will be hard to stick to a healthy diet if your kitchen cupboards are full of unhealthy processed foods. Before you start, have a clear-out and get rid of the things you're no longer going to eat, so that you won't be tempted to indulge. Then you can re-stock your cupboards with healthy, natural ingredients! You'll also need to make regular trips to the shops or farmers' market to keep your fridge stocked with fresh fruit, vegetables and lean meat. On the following page is a shopping list to get you started.

Store cupboard

beans and pulses
(tinned or dry)

brown rice

gluten-free and
wholegrain flours

healthy oils (olive oil,
flaxseed oil, etc)

herbs and spices

lentils

low-salt stock cubes

maple syrup, coconut
sugar or stevia

oats

salt and pepper

wholegrain pasta

Snacks

dried fruit

nuts

seeds

wholegrain crackers

Meat and protein

fish

skinless chicken breast

tofu

turkey mince

Fruits

bananas

berries

citrus fruit

kiwis

mangoes

pomegranate

Vegetables

asparagus

avocado

beansprouts

broccoli

kale

peppers

spinach

sweet potatoes

tomatoes

Milk and dairy

almond milk, oat milk,
rice milk or soya milk

eggs

low-fat cheese

low-fat yoghurt

skimmed milk

Sticking With It

With our busy lives, maintaining a healthy diet can sometimes be a challenge, so it's important to stay motivated. One of the best ways to do this is to focus on the health benefits of your new lifestyle. Within the first week or two you should already start to see the positive effects, such as weight loss, clearer skin, more energy, better digestion and losing those dark circles under your eyes. If you get tempted to revert back to your old ways, take a moment to focus on how much better you feel on your new diet.

Setting goals

Think about what you want to achieve with your new diet. If you write down your goals and targets and post them somewhere you'll see them regularly – such as on the fridge or a kitchen cupboard – you'll be more likely to achieve them. Include ideas like trying at least two new recipes each week, so you don't get stuck in a rut.

Spread the word!

You're not in this alone. Tell your friends and family about your new lifestyle. Even if they don't want to join in, they can still offer support and encouragement. They might want to join you for a brisk walk, or try out some new recipes with you. Be a positive example: offering someone tips and advice for a healthier lifestyle can help keep you motivated, too.

Treat yourself

You deserve a treat for sticking with your new diet, but try to get out of the habit of using food as a reward. Make a chart and plan some non-food rewards for sticking to your diet and exercise targets. These could be a trip to the cinema, coffee with a friend, a massage, a glossy magazine, a new top or even a lazy night in with a box set you've been meaning to watch!

Diet consultant: Jo Stimpson

Written by: Ruth Manning

Main food photography and recipe development:
© Stockfood, The Food Media Agency

Picture Credits:

Dreamstime: Travelbook 8, Johnfoto 10bl, Picsfive 10br, Monkey Business Images 11, 17, 20, Kamil Macniak 15, Summertime08 18, Syda Productions 19, 124, Marilyn Barbone 28, Svetlana Voronina 59, Serhiy Shullye 84, Joystockphoto 91, Yurakp 92, 110, Svetamart 95, Colourdream 98, Yulia Davidovich 101, Zkruger 102, Hyrman 105, Agorulko 106, Baibaz 109, Robyn Mackenzie 113, Melica 123; Shutterstock: Maridav 4, Wavebreakmedia 6, 9, 14, Minerva Studio 12, Goran Bogicevic 13, Vgstudio 23, Goodluz 24, Antpkr 31, Maks Narodenko 32, 39, Kekyalyaynen 35, Nattika 36, 65, Gayvoronskaya_Yana 40, Egor Rodynchenko 44, 66, Volosina 47, 117l, Christian Jung 48, 51, 77, Onair 52, Valentyn Volkov 55, 62, Kovaleva_Ka 56, Binh Thanh Bui 69, Viktar Malyshchyts 70, Tiger Images 73, Madlen 74, 87, Dionisvera 80, Bergamont 83, Matin 88, AVAVA 112, Verca 115, Elena Elisseeva 117r, Igor Dutina 119, Monkey Business Images 122, Racorn 127, Rido 128.